CONTENTS

WELCOME 2

WHO'S WHO 4

EXPLORE 6

This part of the book will help
you discover the main buildings
and features of the castle.

The summit enclosure	8
The upper bailey	10
The water gate & doocot	12
The gatehouse	14
The ditch, causeway & drawbridge	18
The castletoun	20
The nether bailey	21
The great hall	24
The great hall range	26
The Grant buildings	28
The Grant Tower	30

HISTORY 32

This part of the book will
help you discover the stories
behind the castle.

Timeline	34
Airchartdan & Columba	38
Columba & the water beast	40
Changing cultures	42
The estate of Urquhart	44
The castle as a residence	46
Fortunes of war	48
An uneasy peace	50
A kingdom within a kingdom	52
Clash of the clans	54
Linn Nan Creach – 'The Age of Forays'	56
Grand larceny: The Great Raid	58
Highland tradition: Dùthchas	60
The king's enforcers	62
National struggles & local feuds	64
A Highland garrison	66
The 'damnification' of Urquhart	67
A noble ruin	68

Further reading 71
Credits 71

MAP 72

Cover Urquhart Castle in its
dominant position on Loch Ness.
Back cover A brooch found
at the castle, probably dating
from the 1400s.
This spread Medieval nails
found at the castle.

1

WELCOME TO URQUHART CASTLE

Today, the setting of Urquhart Castle is tranquil, with superb views across Loch Ness and the rugged landscape of the Highlands. But this is not just a picturesque ruin. For centuries, this was a busy focus of power in the region, with sporadic episodes of turmoil and bloodshed.

The site has good natural defences, and a timber fort probably stood here in Pictish times (around AD 500–1000).

The stone castle was built in about 1230 by the Durwards, installed by Alexander II to assert royal authority in the region.

The earliest major event we know of at Urquhart was in 1296, when the castle was captured by the invading English army. From the mid-1300s it was a Scottish royal castle, but further bloodshed came in the 1400s and 1500s as Islesmen from the west swept up the Great Glen, initially to assert power and later to plunder.

The final siege was during the Jacobite Rising of 1689–90. When the government troops left in 1693, they supposedly blew up the gatehouse, leaving the castle impossible to defend.

Visitors can now enjoy a peaceful ruin with a long and eventful history.

1 Urquhart Castle viewed from the north.
2 Gaming pieces found at Urquhart.

WHO'S WHO

ST COLUMBA
(521–97)

The Irish priest (*below*) baptised a dying Pictish chieftain at Urquhart around AD 580.

p.38-41

EDWARD I
(1239–1307)

In 1296, the English king (*below*) exploited a crisis in Scotland's royal succession and invaded, capturing many castles including Urquhart.

p.48-50

ALAN DURWARD
(d. around 1270)

One of Scotland's most powerful figures in the mid-1200s, Alan Durward (*coat of arms, above*) was granted the estate of Urquhart around 1230 and probably built the first stone castle on the site.

p.42-5

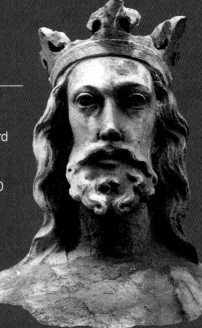

ROBERT THE BRUCE
(1274–1329)

In 1307, Bruce (*above*) led his army up the Great Glen, capturing several strongholds including Urquhart Castle, where he installed a garrison.
p.50

ALEXANDER STEWART, EARL OF BUCHAN
(1343–1405)

'The Wolf of Badenoch' (*right*) gained possession of Urquhart Castle around 1380. He expanded the castle, but may have mismanaged the estate.
p.51

EÒIN MACDONALD, LORD OF THE ISLES AND EARL OF ROSS
(1434–1503)

Eòin succeeded his father in 1449, and two years later, aged just 16, he led his army up the Great Glen to expand his territory. He captured Urquhart, which he held for 25 years.
p.52-3

JOHN GRANT OF FREUCHIE, THE 'RED BARD'
(1468–1528)

After acquiring the estate in 1485, Grant restored some order to unruly Glenurquhart. James IV rewarded him by granting him the lordship and castle.
p.56

MARY GRANT
(c.1595–c.1645)

Born into minor nobility, Mary Ogilvy married Urquhart's laird, Sir John Grant, in 1613 and came to live at the castle after his death in 1637. According to local legend, she was an unpopular landlady, and was finally driven out of the glen.
p.64

EXPLORING THE CASTLE

We recommend that you begin at the summit enclosure, where you'll find the oldest parts of the castle, and end your visit at the Grant Tower, the last major building to be added. But you can explore the ruins in any order you like.

Urquhart Castle sprawls across two mounds on an hourglass-shaped headland, surrounded on three sides by Loch Ness. The setting provides good natural defences, though it is overlooked by higher ground on the landward side to the west.

Urquhart first appears in the historical record in the 500s AD, and the site continued in use until 1693. Its bare rubble walls bear witness to a sometimes turbulent history.

Much of the stonework and architectural detailing has been removed or destroyed. As a result, our ability to interpret the remains of this once magnificent medieval stronghold is limited. Important archaeological discoveries, together with careful reading of the architectural and documentary evidence, have filled in many of the gaps in our knowledge, but much remains open to interpretation.

This page A drawing of Urquhart Castle dating from around 1850.

THE SUMMIT ENCLOSURE

The highest part of the site was probably the earliest to be occupied. It is well defended, with a clear view of Loch Ness and the surrounding landscape.

Some traces of early occupation have been found at the summit. They include vitrified (fused) stone, which points to a prehistoric fort.

Indications of intense heating, which causes rocks to melt and bond, are sometimes found on fortified sites dating from about 500 BC until AD 500. The vitrified stone, combined with radiocarbon dating from timbers excavated in the 1980s, suggests that the site may have been occupied as early as the 500s AD.

The earliest surviving stonework dates to the mid-1200s, and may relate to the acquisition of Urquhart by Alan Durward, a major figure at the court of Alexander II.

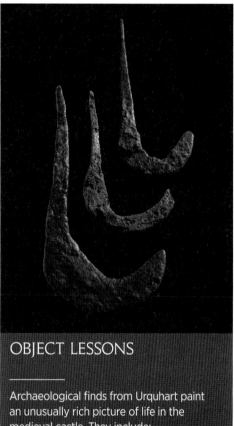

At this time, a stout stone wall was built around the top of the mound at the south of the site ❶. This summit enclosure may have incorporated a small stone tower at one end. The walls protected more vulnerable timber buildings within.

A ditch ❷ was dug to strengthen the defences, and a timber palisade ❸ may have enclosed the rest of the area. In the decades that followed, this was replaced with a stone wall. Meanwhile, the focus of occupation shifted to the northern half of the enclosure.

The summit stronghold continued to be used at times, perhaps as a refuge during the conflict between the Crown and the MacDonald Lords over the earldom of Ross (see page 51).

Many medieval artefacts have been found in the summit enclosure. They provide a valuable insight into castle life and the local economy from the 1200s to the 1400s.

Left An artist's impression of how the castle may have looked in the mid-1200s.

OBJECT LESSONS

Archaeological finds from Urquhart paint an unusually rich picture of life in the medieval castle. They include:

- Pruning knives (*above*) – used to tend to the castle's food crops.
- Kitchen knives (p.27) – evidence of the large number of residents catered for.
- Gaming pieces (p.3) – a simple indication of leisure pursuits.
- Horseshoes and spurs (p.11) – a reminder that horses were kept at the castle.
- Arrowheads (p.49) – a grim reminder of the castle's long history of violence.

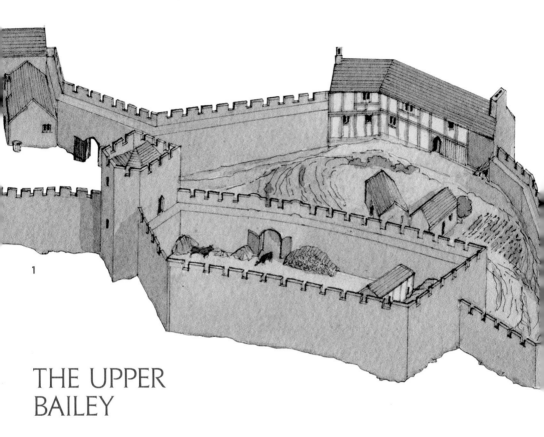

1

THE UPPER BAILEY

The area of the castle below the summit enclosure is known as the upper bailey, and would have held important secondary buildings. As the castle developed, the residential focus shifted to the northern half of the enclosure. At that point, this area probably became a service close, containing more functional buildings.

Facilities for everyday life in the castle were probably sited here, in buildings largely built from timber. These may have included:

BAKERY   BREWERY   STABLES

1 The upper bailey as it may have
   looked around 1350.

This area continued to serve the castle's practical requirements into the 1500s.

A smithy?

The ruin of a large building stands on the lochside below the summit enclosure. It was probably built in the 1300s, but very few features survive to tell us how it was used. At one point it may have been a smithy, where blacksmiths made and repaired tools, weapons and horseshoes.

Timber slots survive in the west wall, and like many of the buildings at Urquhart, it may have been partly constructed from wood. There were ample supplies of timber available locally.

2 Medieval horseshoes found at the castle.
3 A spur found at the castle, probably dating from the 1400s.

THE WATER GATE & DOOCOT

The water gate

At the narrow waist of the hourglass-shaped site, opposite the gatehouse, is the water gate. This gave access to the loch shore and was an important point of entry in medieval times.

In an age when roads were easily rendered impassable, provisions would have come by boat and been offloaded below the water gate. Timber and furs for trading would have travelled to Inverness by the same route.

North of the water gate are the ruins of a small building attached to the kitchen, which opens onto the loch. This may have been used for net storage or boat repairs.

Between this store and the water gate is the footprint of another building. This might have been a stable, where guests dismounted after entering the courtyard through the gatehouse.

1 The water gate.
2 The doocot.

2

The doocot

The circular structure below the summit enclosure was a doocot – or dovecote. Positioned in a quiet area of the castle, it is almost certainly the 'dove-grove' referred to in a charter of 1509.

Designed as safe housing for pigeons, doocots were common features in medieval castles, providing a regular supply of meat and eggs. Four nesting-boxes survive.

PLENTY OF FISH

Loch Ness was important in providing food for the residents – not just as a source of fish but also as a transport route.

Although freshwater fish was eaten here, saltwater fish was preferred. Cod, haddock and pollack were brought in from Inverness, perhaps dried or salted. Choosing to buy fish, rather than catching it locally, may have been a display of wealth.

Below Medieval illustration of fishermen at work.

THE GATEHOUSE

This formidable structure was the main entrance to the castle. It allowed access to be controlled, and provided accommodation for an important member of castle staff.

The gatehouse controlled entry into the castle. It also included a lodging for the keeper, who was responsible for the daily running, maintenance and defence of the castle. From here, he could control admission to the site.

The gatehouse was remodelled repeatedly over centuries of use, but eventually suffered severe damage, supposedly soon after the Jacobite Rising of 1689. Troops loyal to the joint monarchs William and Mary were then stationed here. Legend says that when they abandoned the castle in 1693, they blew up the gatehouse. But no historical sources support this story. It may just be a tradition inspired by the ruined tower fragments.

Some remains of the upper rooms lie on the grass beside the gatehouse; they include chimney flues.

Right The gatehouse.

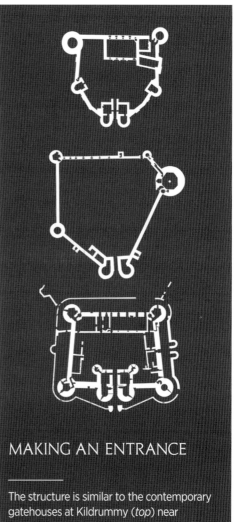

MAKING AN ENTRANCE

The structure is similar to the contemporary gatehouses at Kildrummy (*top*) near Aberdeen and Bothwell (*middle*) near Glasgow, but also at Harlech (*bottom*) in Wales. All of these examples can be dated to the late 1200s or early 1300s, the period when Urquhart's gatehouse was probably built.

❶ Entrance passage
Wide enough to allow carts to pass through and strongly defended.

❷ Portcullis
This grating of bars protected the entrance passage, and was raised and lowered from an upper floor. The grooves that held it in place can still be seen.

❸ Inner barrier
These would either be stout timber doors or iron grilles called yetts.

❹ Winding house
This room housed the winding mechanism for the portcullis. It also gave access to a room high above the outer portal.

❺ Murder holes
These allowed defenders to hurl objects down on intruders, who could be trapped between the portcullis and the inner barrier.

❻ Porter's lodge
The porter checked visitors' credentials during the day and ensured the castle was securely locked and barred at night. He rang a bell at the top of the gatehouse to signify the 'hours' dividing up the household's day and signalled the change in the night watch.

❼ Prison cell
Prisoners awaiting trial were held here, within the porter's lodge.

❽ Keeper's lodge
Now reached by a modern spiral stair, this lodging was probably occupied by the keeper: from here he controlled access into the castle. It comprises a hall (reception room) and a private chamber with a large bed recess. Both rooms had fireplaces and latrines.

❾ South gatehouse lodge
This lodge is entered from the courtyard. It was later converted into a kiln-house, where corn was dried and stored.

THE GATEHOUSE – WHAT TO LOOK FOR

THE DITCH, CAUSEWAY AND DRAWBRIDGE

From the top of the gatehouse you can get a good view of the great ditch which defends the landward side of the castle. Just beyond this lay the castletoun – a cluster of buildings between the castle itself and the higher ground where the visitor centre now stands (see page 20).

The ditch

This first line of defence is thought to have been dug in the early or mid-1200s, though this has never been confirmed by archaeological study.

The ditch was hacked out of solid rock, dividing the castle's headland from the broad, open terrace to the west. It was designed to protect the landward side of the castle, which was vulnerable to attack.

1

The causeway and drawbridge

The ditch was partially bridged by a stone causeway, much of which survives. The remaining gap was spanned by a drawbridge that could be raised to prevent intruders crossing. This has been replaced by a modern fixed bridge.

The medieval drawbridge would have been a heavy and robust timber structure. It was operated from the castle side of the ditch using a timber superstructure that has long since disappeared. Large vertical sockets for its uprights survive in the stone foundations on the castle side of the ditch.

You can still see stone buttresses on both sides of the ditch. These were designed to counteract the immense thrust of the timbers and the lifting mechanism.

High stone walls enclosed the inner part of the causeway, between the drawbridge and gatehouse. Now reduced to ruins, they were equipped with arrow-slits and two gates, or sallyports, via which the garrison could exit to attack the enemy while the drawbridge remained locked and barred.

1 The ditch and causeway.
2 Lowering the drawbridge to allow visitors into the castle.

THE CASTLETOUN

Beyond the ditch was the castletoun,
a noisy, industrious settlement filled with
tanners, woodworkers, metalworkers
and more. The remains of Urquhart's
castletoun were found when archaeologists
investigated the site of the visitor centre
before it was constructed.

1 An iron key found at the castle.
2 Medieval blacksmiths at work.

1

2

THE NETHER BAILEY

At some point in the later 1200s, the heart of the castle shifted to the northern half of the headland.

It was probably around this time that the stone curtain wall was completed, with the gatehouse at its main entrance.

It is likely that the lord's grand lodgings, great hall and kitchen were also part of this building scheme. However, we cannot be sure when these features were constructed.

By 1275, Alan Durward died without a male heir. The lordship passed to his daughter, Ermengarde, and soon afterwards to her son, Nicholas de Soules, Lord of Liddesdale.

In the centuries after Durward's death, these buildings were repeatedly modified and added to, but there is very little evidence to help us date this work. It is also difficult to be sure who was controlling the castle in the later 1200s, and why repairs or new buildings were commissioned.

Aside from the gatehouse, they have all been reduced to foundations and low walls.

3 A view over the nether bailey from the southern part of the castle.

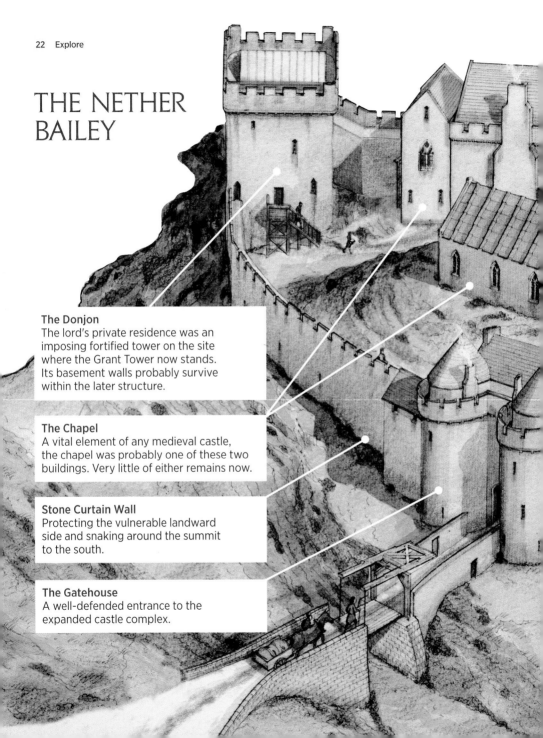

THE NETHER BAILEY

The Donjon
The lord's private residence was an imposing fortified tower on the site where the Grant Tower now stands. Its basement walls probably survive within the later structure.

The Chapel
A vital element of any medieval castle, the chapel was probably one of these two buildings. Very little of either remains now.

Stone Curtain Wall
Protecting the vulnerable landward side and snaking around the summit to the south.

The Gatehouse
A well-defended entrance to the expanded castle complex.

The Great Kitchen
Built as an extension to the great hall for the preparation of banquets.

The Great Hall
A large chamber facing out over the loch, used for hosting banquets, managing the estate and dispensing justice. The scale and grandeur of this building proclaimed the high social standing of the castle's owner.

Chamber
An extension to the great hall providing more private rooms for the lord and lady.

THE GREAT HALL

Facing the loch is a crescent-shaped row of rectangular structures, with the great hall at its centre. Probably built in the later 1200s, this would have been one of the grandest ranges of buildings in Scotland at the time.

The **great hall** was the main living space, with several functions. It was used by the castle's owners for feasting, administration of the estate and dispensing justice. It was also used by household staff for:

EATING   **SOCIALISING**   **SLEEPING**

The lord and his family would have had private chambers elsewhere in the castle.

The only part that now survives is the basement. It contains what may be a masonry support for the base of a central hearth in the timber-floored hall above.

THE GREAT HALL RANGE

The **great chamber** was built at the north end of the great hall. This was a comfortable, more private space to which the lord and his lady could retire. A similar room was provided in many castles of this period.

The **chamber** had thinner walls than the hall and, like most of Urquhart's buildings, made good use of timber in its construction. Only the basement walls survive today, but you can see the slots in them that once held timbers to support the floor above.

1 A view over the castle from the Grant Tower,
  with the ruins of the great hall range on the left.
2 Kitchen knives found at the site.

2

The **great kitchens** were at the south end of the great hall. Only fragments survive, including the water inlet, the small rectangular opening at the side of the walkway. Water from the loch would be carried up here in pails for use in the kitchen. The central doorway, flanked by two windows, leads into the basement from the courtyard.

Food would have been carried upstairs, probably into a servery next to the hall.

Later adaptation

At some point in the later Middle Ages, the great hall range was substantially redeveloped. This suggests a change in the way the buildings were used, and may reflect a change in ownership.

At this time, the chamber must have fallen out of use as a high-status apartment: a latrine from the remodelled hall now emptied into its basement.

THE URQUHART EWER

This fine bronze ewer was found at the castle in 1921 and was affectionately called 'the Teapot'. It was probably made in the 1400s and once had a hinged lid. It would have been used for washing hands over a flat-bottomed bowl. It is now on display in the castle exhibition.

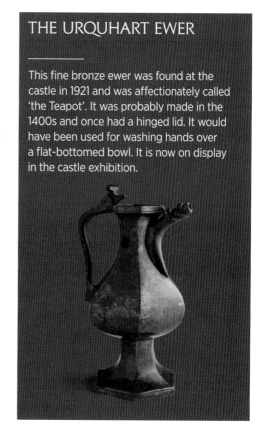

1

THE GRANT BUILDINGS

In December 1509 James IV gave the lordship of Urquhart to John Grant of Freuchie. He and his descendants built the last of the castle's major buildings, including the Grant Tower.

The royal charter required Grant to 'repair, build or else construct a tower ... from stone and lime', to ensure that the castle was properly defended. Other buildings on the site were also to be repaired or built. But in any case he would presumably have wanted to upgrade them according to the fashions and requirements of the day.

At some point in the 1500s, a new tower house was built on the footprint of the donjon at the northern end of the headland (see page 30). This was clearly the work of the Grant family, though we cannot be sure exactly when it was begun or completed.

1 A kitchen of the 1500s.
2 The Grant buildings today.

The basement of the old tower was buried to create a level surface. A small cobbled courtyard or close was formed around the new tower, and this was walled off from the nether bailey. Two other buildings were accessed from this new close.

The building to the west of the Grant Tower has small fireplaces at both ends, indicating that it was divided in two. It may have been a kitchen, but the size of the fireplaces makes this unlikely.

The building to the south of the Grant Tower has a basement that was probably a storeroom. It was built on the site of an earlier structure adjoining the great hall range. This may have been the castle chapel but no clear evidence survives.

A fragment of walling between this building and the tower may have been part of a bread oven, suggesting that a kitchen stood here at some point.

THE GRANT TOWER

The Grant Tower consists of five storeys, connected by spiral stairs. Although partially ruined, it retains much of its sense of space and grandeur.

Part of the south wall has collapsed, probably during a 'storme of wind' in February 1715.

❶ Entrance
Leading into the hall at courtyard level.

❷ Hall
An outer reception room where visitors could be received, whether or not they were permitted into the more private chambers above. Lit by good-sized windows and heated by a large fireplace, it may also have been used for dining.

❸ Storeroom
Reached via a narrow spiral stair, this stone-vaulted chamber has a well-defended postern, or back entry. The thick walls were probably part of the medieval donjon, a residential tower that once stood on the same site.

❹ Private chamber
This fine room was a private chamber where the Grants could dine and entertain in greater privacy, with their closest friends and advisors.

❺ Bed chamber
This was also a reception room, reserved for the Grants' most intimate companions. It would also have contained an elaborate bed.

❻ Parapets
These were the handiwork of James Murray, master mason, who carried out major repairs at the castle in 1623.

❼ Garret
A small room at the top of the tower, perhaps used by minor members of the family.

❽ Square-gabled turrets
Each contains a little chamber with a fireplace and a window giving a magnificent view of the glen.

Left The Grant Tower as it may have looked in the 1600s.

HISTORY OF THE CASTLE

The very extensive lands of Urquhart, with their castle perched on a dramatic headland, occupy a key strategic location in Scotland.

Known in Gaelic as Caisteal Urchadain or Caisteal na Sròine ('the Castle on the Headland'), Urquhart Castle stands on the north-west coast of Loch Ness. From this position, it controlled traffic through the Great Glen, a key route between the east and west.

As a result it has been embroiled in many conflicts, including the Wars of Independence and persistent, bitter clan feuds. Its very long story reflects the history of Scotland and its people over a long period.

Right A bronze brooch found at the castle, dating from the 1300s or 1400s.

TIMELINE 500–1371

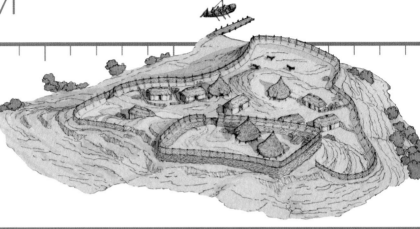

Around 500
—
A **Pictish hillfort**, *right*, is probably established on the summit.

1230s
—
Sir Alan Durward gains the lordship. In the next few years he probably builds the first stone castle at Urquhart, and marries the king's daughter Marjorie.

1275
—
Durward, *coat of arms left*, dies without an heir and the estate of Urquhart passes to the de Soules family, via his daughter Ermengarde.

1307
—
King Robert the Bruce, *left*, probably recaptures Urquhart Castle, which he places under the control of his nephew Thomas Randolph.

1312
—
Bruce makes Randolph Earl of Moray and gives him the barony of Urquhart.

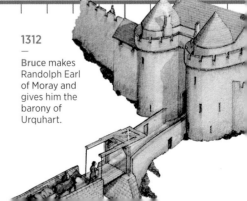

Around 580
—
St Columba, *right*, travels from Iona to Inverness, stopping on his way to baptise a Pictish chief at Airchartdan – probably Urquhart.

Around 1000
—
The Pictish hillfort at Urquhart is thought to have been destroyed by fire, based on the discovery of cracked and fused stonework at the site.

1296
—
Edward I, *left*, invades Scotland and captures many strongholds, including Urquhart Castle.

1297
—
Sir Andrew Murray, *coat of arms left*, besieges the castle but initially fails to capture it from the English.

1330s
—
Urquhart Castle is one of very few strongholds to remain in Scottish hands during the Second War of Independence.

1371
—
Robert Stewart, *right*, grandson of Robert the Bruce, becomes King of Scots, beginning the long line of Stewart monarchs.

TIMELINE
1384–1692

1384
—
Alexander Stewart,
Earl of Buchan, *right*,
known as 'The Wolf
of Badenoch',
gains ownership
of Urquhart Castle.

1450s
—
Eòin MacDonald,
Lord of the Isles
leads a rising against
James II, *right*, and
seizes Urquhart
Castle. The politically
vulnerable king allows
him to keep it.

1513
—
The Battle of Flodden,
Northumberland.
James IV is killed
with many of his
followers, weakening
royal control of the
Highlands.

1644
—
Mary Grant,
coat of arms left,
is supposedly driven
out of the glen, having
survived years of
local conflict between
Covenanting and
Royalist forces.

1689
—
Ludovic Grant,
8th Laird raises a
regiment to resist the
first Jacobite Rising,
stationing troops at
Urquhart Castle and
other strongholds.
In December they fight
off a Jacobite attack.

Around 1480

George Gordon,
2nd Earl of Huntly
leases Urquhart to
Sir Duncan Grant of
Freuchie. The Grants
will hold the castle
for nearly 200 years.

1509

James IV, *right,* awards
the Grants the lordship
of Urquhart.

1545

The Great Raid, the
worst of many attacks
on Urquhart by marauding
Islesmen led by the
MacDonalds. Vast amounts
of livestock, crops,
furniture, money and
other goods are stolen
from the estate.

1637

James Grant, *left,*
becomes 7th laird
of Freuchie and
installs his widowed
mother Mary Grant
at Urquhart Castle.

1693

Troops depart from the
castle after several years,
supposedly blowing up
the gatehouse, *right.* Grant
demands compensation
for their 'damnifying'
of his property.

1912

Urquhart Castle is placed in State
care. Clearance work carried out
after the First World War (1914–18)
produces a large collection of finds.
Excavation and research continue
to the present day, improving our
understanding of this unique site.

AIRCHARTDAN & COLUMBA

The first written reference to the lands of Urquhart appears in St Adomnán's *Life of St Columba*, written in the late 600s. The name means 'by the wood or thicket'.

Around AD 580, St Columba travelled through the Great Glen on a long and arduous journey to the court of Bridei, king of the Picts, at Inverness.

Adomnán tells us that he stopped at a place called Airchartdan or Urquhart. While there he baptised Emchath, a dying man who had 'preserved his natural goodness all through his life'. Not only Emchath but his whole household were baptised. When the ceremony was complete, Emchath 'gladly and confidently departed to the Lord'.

Urquhart was a vast area of land, and we cannot be sure that Emchath's residence was on the headland where the castle now stands. However, the discovery here of a fragment of Pictish brooch has led to speculation that his residence was in much the same position.

1

1 Columba as depicted in stained glass at Iona Abbey.

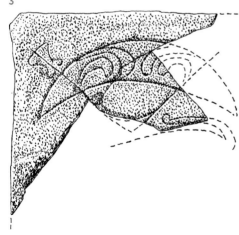

Archaeologists have discovered evidence that this was a well-fortified place around Columba's time (see page 8). It was certainly an ideal site for a fort, surrounded on three sides by the deep waters of the loch, easily defended from the landward side and commanding extensive views.

Other missionaries followed in the footsteps of Columba, and the existing landscape of sacred sites was gradually Christianised. An incised cross dating from Pictish times has been found at Temple, on the north side of Urquhart Bay, whose name is an anglicised form of *an teampull*, ('chapel').

2 A fragment of a Pictish silver brooch found near the castle.
3 An illustration of a Pictish carved stone found at Garbeg Farm, near Urquhart.

COLUMBA &
THE WATER BEAST

Today, many people visit this area to
try to catch a glimpse of the legendary
'Loch Ness Monster'. Tales of water beasts
have long been associated with Highland
lochs. But the sighting of a monster in
or near Loch Ness was first recorded
in Adomnán's biography of Columba,
written around AD 700.

The episode is described as follows:

'When the blessed man stayed for some
days in the land of the Picts, he had to
cross the River Ness. When he reached
its bank, he saw some of the local people
burying a poor fellow. They said they had
seen a water beast snatch him and maul
him savagely as he was swimming not long
before ... The blessed man, having been
told all this, astonished them by sending
one of his companions to swim across the
river and sail back to him in a dinghy that
was on the further bank ...

'Luigne moccu Min obeyed without
hesitation. He took off his clothes except
for a tunic and dived into the water.
But the beast was lying low on the riverbed,
its appetite not so much sated as whetted
for prey. It could sense that the water above
was stirred by the swimmer, and suddenly
swam up to the surface, rushing open-
mouthed with a great roar towards the
man ... [Columba] looking on raised his
holy hand and made the sign of the cross
in the air, and invoking the name of God,
he commanded the fierce beast, saying:
*"Go no further. Do not touch the man.
Go back at once."*

'At the sound of the saint's voice, the
beast fled in terror so fast one might have
thought it was pulled back with ropes ...
The brethren were amazed to see that the
beast had gone and that their fellow-soldier
Luigne returned to them untouched and
safe in the dinghy, and they glorified God
in the blessed man.'

Right St Columba as depicted in stained glass
at St Margaret's Chapel in Edinburgh Castle.

CHANGING CULTURES

The story of Urquhart Castle is closely linked to the families who owned it over several centuries. Their origins and development reflect wider changes that were occurring in Scotland.

The first historical references to a castle at Urquhart date from the early 1200s.

The Durwards are the first recorded lords of Urquhart, and Alan Durward probably built the earliest parts of Urquhart Castle. At that time, Scotland was largely Gaelic-speaking, as was its royal court.

Durward came from a prominent Gaelic family, with claims across north-east Scotland. He was also son-in-law to King Alexander II, having married his daughter Marjorie.

1

As a powerful lord, Alan Durward had his own household of retainers. One of them was a man called Gilbert, who was 'Seneschal of Urquhart', the steward of the Durward household. Records suggest Gilbert was known as Gille Ruaidh ('The Red-Haired Lad').

Urquhart was in royal ownership, and was granted to a succession of influential lords in the medieval period. These included the Stewart earls of Buchan, who spent over a century warring with rival lords for control of territory in the Highlands.

In 1485, the castle would be rented to James Grant of Freuchie. The Grants were likely Norman in origin, with the name originating from the French *grand*, meaning 'great'. However, the Grants were keen to emphasise their Gaelic origins. They traced their family to the Sìol Ailpein kin-group and thus to the first king of Scots, Cinead mac Ailpìn (Kenneth MacAlpin).

Grant of Freuchie presented himself as a Highland chief, amassing the trappings of a Gaelic court. Unusually, he is recorded as having both a piper and a clàrsach (harp) player.

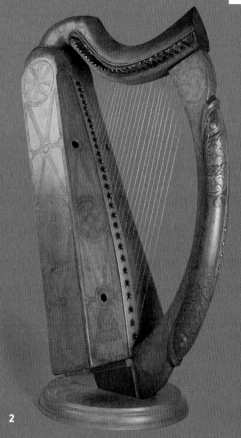

2

These were separate musical traditions in Gaelic culture of the time, and only wealthy chiefs could support both. Grant also performed another important role of the Highland chief – engaging in clan warfare.

The shifting ownership between monarchs, Scottish-Norman earls and Gaelic chiefs at Urquhart reflects the medieval kingdom of the Scots as a whole – there were multiple cultures, identities and loyalties.

1 Alan Durward, accompanied by his steward Gille Ruaidh, meets local landowners as he exerts control over Urquhart.

2 A replica clàrsach, or Gaelic harp. This instrument was an important element of Highland culture in medieval times.

1

THE ESTATE OF URQUHART

Urquhart Castle was the centre of a vast estate reaching from Loch Ness to the mountains far to the west.

We have no details of the extent of the estate granted to the Durwards in the 1220s. However, royal charters survive from 1509, providing an accurate picture of the lordship at that time, including its extent and the settlements within it.

It included both Glen Urquhart and Glen Moriston to its south, and extended from the fertile cornlands beside Loch Ness, inland over good pasture to the rich hunting grounds of the Cluny Forest, high in the mountains to the west.

The parish of Glen Urquhart and Glen Moriston probably corresponded with the estate boundary. The parish had a single church at Kilmore as its focus, but in a parish of this size other holy sites were also needed, to serve a dispersed population.

1   Glen Urquhart.
2   A wild stag. Hunting deer was a popular pursuit for medieval nobles.

These included the main church in the vicinity, St Ninian's near Drumnadrochit, which also housed relics, a shrine and a holy well.

The medieval castle was closely connected with the surrounding estate. The lord's own demesne, or domain, was located at Borlum, on the higher ground overlooking the castle to the west – this land was retained to support him and his household. The name comes from 'boardland', meaning 'land for the lord's table'.

Urquhart had access to one of the best hunting reserves in Scotland, the royal forest of Cluny, which the lord of Urquhart administered on his sovereign's behalf. Many deer bones were found during archaeological excavations at Urquhart.

Hunting was an important social activity for nobility, imbued with cultural meaning, but deer were also important economically. They provided meat, hides and antler to be used by residents of the castle, or sold at the markets in the burgh of Inverness.

Good pastureland also supported large numbers of cattle. A herd of cattle was both a status symbol for the lords of Urquhart – and clan chiefs – and an essential commodity, providing meat and dairy. The estate also had valuable woodlands, providing timber to trade at Inverness.

2

THE CASTLE AS A RESIDENCE

Urquhart Castle was a major settlement: not only a stronghold but also a civic centre, estate office, military base, law court and prison.

In its 400-year history, the castle was never the main residence of the families who possessed it. The chief seat of the Durwards was at Coull, and the Grants, who held Urquhart in later years, resided mainly at Freuchie (now Castle Grant) beside Grantown-on-Spey.

For most of the intervening years, Urquhart was a royal castle, though no kings or queens ever slept here.

The castle would normally have been overseen by a keeper, who was responsible for fortifying and maintaining it.

He had to recruit a garrison of armed men, keep the household supplied with provisions and give military service to the Crown when required.

1 This ceramic fragment, modelled as a comical face, was found at the site. It was part of a medieval 'knight's jug'. A replica jug is displayed alongside it, giving an idea of its overall appearance when complete.

2 The keeper's lodging was in the upper floor of the gatehouse.

3 Like any large medieval stronghold, Urquhart Castle had substantial cellar space for storage of provisions, often paid to the lord as rent.

The keepers of Urquhart played an important role in the 1300s. It was a turbulent century, and the keepers changed less frequently than the owners.

Sir Robert Lauder held the castle against the English in 1334 and remained keeper until he was succeeded by his grandson in the 1350s or 60s. The Lauders were a well-established local family who brought stability to the castle and its estate for several generations.

Usually, the keeper worked closely with the steward, whose job was to run the household and manage the estate. However, there are no references to a steward at Urquhart, and it seems likely that in this case the two roles were combined.

Medieval lords were constantly on the move, attending their king and sittings of Parliament, visiting their peers and waging war at home and overseas. They also had to visit their estates to dispense justice and consume their rents, most of which were paid in kind (crops and livestock) rather than cash.

Wherever the lord went, he was accompanied by his retinue. Evidence from elsewhere in Scotland suggests that the lord of Urquhart kept a household of well over 100 people. Most of his furniture and furnishings would have travelled with them too.

When the lord was in residence at Urquhart, the castle would have been crowded, warm and noisy. At other times, it would have been largely empty.

3

FORTUNES OF WAR

When the Wars of Independence broke out in the late 1200s, Urquhart Castle was soon embroiled in this great conflict.

The wars arose from a succession crisis. In 1290, the seven-year-old Queen Margaret died on her way to Scotland from Norway, ending the line of Gaelic monarchs from the house of Canmore.

Edward I of England was invited to arbitrate between several candidates to succeed her, and endorsed John Balliol, Lord of Galloway, who had the strongest claim to the throne. However, Edward demanded obedience from the new Scottish king, and in 1295, John and his nobles rebelled. The following year, Edward invaded Scotland, defeating King John, who was forced to abdicate.

Edward's forces advanced into Scotland, capturing many castles. Urquhart was among them, a bitter loss for the Scots. It occupied a crucial position – a place of great defensive strength and located on the Great Glan, a key route through the Highlands connecting north-east and western Scotland.

As early as 1297 the Scots launched their first major attack against Edward. Sir Andrew Murray, a powerful nobleman, led a campaign in the north and had his sights set on Urquhart.

Murray and a group of Scottish knights besieged the castle in late May 1297, with a night attack against the English garrison.

1   An illustration of battle, from a medieval manuscript.

Sir William FitzWarine, constable of Urquhart Castle, wrote to Edward: 'Andrew de Moray [Murray] and Alexander Pilchys with their abettors besieged [Urquhart] castle ... William Puer and the writer's son were killed.'

Murray's initial attack was unsuccessful, but Scottish resistance and the threat to the English-held castle remained strong. By September of that year FitzWarine abandoned Urquhart and before long it was back in Scottish hands.

English forces returned to the area in 1303 as Edward I led another campaign north. Earlier historians suggest Edward besieged the castle, though there is no physical or documentary evidence for this. It is more likely those controlling the castle had sided with the English by this time, so Urquhart may have been taken with little force. By 1304, Sir Alexander Comyn of Buchan was acting as constable at Urquhart. The powerful Comyns had by then agreed a peace with the English king.

Soon after this, Robert the Bruce asserted his own claim on the throne: in 1306 he murdered John Comyn, a kinsman of Alexander, and claimed the crown. After Edward I's death in 1307, Bruce took the chance to overthrow his enemies. He swept up the Great Glen, seizing Comyn strongholds as he went. Urquhart was among the castles that fell to Bruce's army, and he awarded it to his loyal nephew Thomas Randolph.

2 Medieval arrowhead found at the castle.
3 The conquering English king, Edward I.

AN UNEASY PEACE

The Wars of Independence dragged on for six decades, but remarkably Urquhart was not directly affected again. Yet it was frequently caught between local and national power struggles.

Initially, Urquhart remained a royal castle, managed by a series of keepers. Sir Robert Lauder successfully held the castle through the 1330s, when Urquhart was one of just a handful of castles to remain in Scottish control. By the 1360s he was succeeded by his grandson, Sir Robert Chisholm.

By 1384, the castle and lordship had passed to Alexander Stewart, Earl of Buchan, younger brother of King Robert II. Known for his volatile temper, he earned the nickname the 'Wolf of Badenoch', and clashed with local magnates such as the Bishop of Elgin and the Dunbar earls of Moray, and possibly even with the Chisholm family.

The earldom of Ross, a huge Highland territory stretching from coast to coast, became the subject of rival claims. Buchan was married to Euphemia, Countess of Ross, and therefore had a claim on the land.

This was challenged by his brothers, the earls of Strathearn and Fife – and by Euphemia herself, who began divorce proceedings in 1391.

The MacDonalds, Lords of the Isles, had interests in this territory too. The extent of their influence and expansion into this area in the 1300s remains open to debate, but they were certainly active along the Great Glen. The following centuries would see Clan Donald drawn into direct conflict around Urquhart.

Despite such power struggles, the Chisholms brought stability, remaining keepers of Urquhart Castle throughout.

The extent to which Urquhart Castle was directly affected by such political turmoil is uncertain. In fact, the wealth of archaeological finds suggest castle life was at its peak during the 1200s and 1300s.

1   The coat of arms of Sir Robert Chisholm, keeper of Urquhart Castle from the 1360s.
2   A map of the 1600s shows the strategic position of Urquhart on the Great Glen.

HISTORIC SCOTLAND
ALBA AOSMHOR

Thank you for visiting.

Save money on entry to other Historic Scotland attractions with Annual Membership or an Explorer Pass and get FREE entry to over 70 attractions in Scotland.

For more information visit:

www.historicenvironment.scot

HISTORIC SCOTLAND
ALBA AOSMHOR

Claigan
Baile
Strath
Carron
Kean cast
Balnogowi cast
Tayne
Fern
Nyg
Foulis cast
Hills of Allabaster of Roſſe
Cromarty
Roſermaſh
ROSSE
Dingwall
Chanonry
Ardmanoth
Red cast
Bewly Abbay
Kair
Aryrſeir
Tornn
Narden
Louet cast
Lein
Invernes
Kylrae cast
Urquhart cast
Neſſa fl
Calder cast
Soilles
Tray
Glennen Urquhart
MVRAY
Bean cast
Lochnes Moyn
Findorne fl
Ranue
Tala
The Lake of Neſſa nor ye river Neſſa are never froſne
Thalen fl
La Garve
Kinguſy
Spey fl
Grampius Mountain
Ellan Moy
Carry
Louth
Ruven
Crumen fl
Frith fl
L. Loyne
Leanny
Badgenoth
Eſſerlothea
Spanza fl
Scarſchioc
Badgenoth
Lough Aber Hilles
L. Loche
L. Gar
Blaire cast
L. Spey
Ranoch
ATHOLE
Inn

A KINGDOM WITHIN A KINGDOM

The 1300s and 1400s saw the Lords of the Isles emerge as a Gaelic power to rival the Scottish Crown. This set the scene for a battle for Scotland's identity – and brought war to Urquhart.

During the Wars of Independence, one of Robert the Bruce's staunchest allies had been Aonghus Òg ('Young Angus'), head of Clan Donald. Aonghus was rewarded with lands in Lochaber.

He also married well, to an Irish princess, Ainé Ní Chatháin, who brought him a retinue of scholars and skilled warriors. Their son Eòin greatly expanded Clan Donald territory through marriage and royal patronage. By 1336, Eòin had assumed the title Rìgh Innse Gall ('Lord of the Isles').

By about 1400 the lordship absorbed most of western Scotland and parts of Ireland. It had an army to rival the Scots Crown, and was making international treaties. Its capital, at Finlaggan on Islay, had all the trappings of a royal court, with lawyers, doctors, musicians and poets, and poetry and music schools.

1 Typical graveslabs of West Highland warriors.
   These examples are from Iona.
2 A warrior in the service of the Lords of the Isles.

3 An illustration of Clan Donald
   mercenaries by Albrecht Dürer.
4 Victorian illustration of the
   Lord of the Isles.

The castle and lands of Urquhart became a
key battleground in the struggle between
this powerful Gaelic lordship and forces
allied to the Scottish royal court.

Domhnall, Lord of the Isles, laid claim to
the vast earldom of Ross through marriage,
and in 1411 pressed this claim by taking
thousands of men to the Battle of Harlaw,
which ended in a bloody stalemate.

In 1431 an army led by Domhnall Ballach,
head of Clann Eòin Mòr (the MacDonalds
of Antrim), defeated King James I's forces
at Inverlochy. By the mid-1430s, Clan Donald
had taken control of the lands of Urquhart.
However, the castle remained loyal to
the Crown.

Domhnall's son Eòin inherited the Lordship
of the Isles in 1449, and soon became
embroiled in courtly intrigue. In 1451,
aged just 16, he led a revolt against King
James II and captured Urquhart. By 1456,
Clan Donald control of the castle was
officially recognised by the Crown.

CLASH OF
THE CLANS

Power struggles between rival clans were common in many parts of Scotland at this time, and were a frequent feature of life in the Great Glen.

There are five designated battlefields along the glen's length, ranging from the Battle of Inverlochy in 1431 to Maol Ruadh in 1688, known as the 'last clan battle'.

Much of this conflict was between Clan Donald and its supporters the Camerons, Clanchattan and MacIntosh one on side, and Clan Gordon (the earls of Huntly) and their supporters the Frasers and Grants on the other.

In fact, the greatest showdown between these factions came in 1690 at the Battle of Cromdale, 30 miles east of the Great Glen. Although the first Jacobite Rising provided a pretext for violence, the roots of this conflict lay in long-running feuds.

A TREASONOUS PACT

Both Scotland and England tried to use Clan Donald influence in Ireland to their advantage. This led to secret plans for rebellion.

In 1462 Eòin, Lord of the Isles, signed the 'Ardtornish–Westminster Treaty' with Edward IV of England *(above, left)* and exiled Scottish lords. This was an agreement to support an English invasion of Scotland and then divide up control of the country.

In the end, this secret treaty came to nothing, but in 1475 James III *(above, right)* decided to use it as ammunition against his rival. He marched an army down the Great Glen, forcing Eòin to accept lower status and the forfeiture of much of his land. Some of it was given to his wife, Elizabeth Livingston, who had left him to live in the household of James's wife Queen Margaret. Urquhart Castle came back into royal control, passing to George Gordon, Earl of Huntly, a rival of Clan Donald.

Clan Donald territories

Clan battles fought in and around the Great Glen

LINN NAN CREACH – 'THE AGE OF FORAYS'

In the late 1400s, Clan Donald collapsed, bringing chaos. From this turmoil arose the clan system as we understand it today. Many Highland clans emerged, some becoming famous and powerful. These included the Grants of Freuchie, who would control Urquhart Castle until its abandonment.

Around 1482, the Earl of Huntly granted the lands and castle of Urquhart to one of his loyal allies, John Grant of Freuchie, known as 'am Bard Ruadh' ('the Red Bard'). As well as paying duty to the king and providing military service, Grant was required to repair or rebuild the castle's main residential tower, ensuring that it could be defended against attack, as well as upgrading other parts of the castle.

From his new position, Grant 'should secure good rule' and stability in the area. However, years of violence and pillage followed.

1　A carved stone from Iona depicting a birlinn, the highly manoeuvrable vessel used by Clan Donald raiders.

1

2

In 1493, James IV declared the Lordship of the Isles forfeit. This created a power vacuum that led to Linn nan Creach – 'the Age of Forays'. In this period, there were seven revolts aimed at restoring the lordship. The violence spilled out of the Highlands into the Lowlands, and even into Ireland.

Other kin-groups were quick to exploit the perceived weakness of Clan Donald. This violent fragmentation arguably saw the emergence of the 'clan system' as we understand it today. Families such as the Campbells grew more powerful as Clan Donald declined. The Earl of Huntly, chief of Clan Gordon, played clans off against each other – and the Crown.

In 1513, James IV was killed at Flodden, ushering in a long period of instability for the Scottish Crown. In the decades that followed, three infants inherited the throne. For much of the century, the monarch was a minor, so Scotland was governed by a string of regents.

Clan Donald took advantage of the Flodden crisis to invade Urquhart, capturing the castle and raiding the surrounding area. Meanwhile, different factions in Scotland and England supported competing claimants to the Clan Donald lordship, further deepening the chaos.

In 1528, when this upheaval was at its height, the Grant chiefdom was inherited by Seumas nan Creach ('James of the Raids') – so named because of the times in which he lived. The lands of Urquhart and the castle were raided by Clan Donald in 1543, but worse was to follow.

2 A claymore, or two-handed Highland
   sword, dating from the early 1500s.

'ABUSION OF JUSTICE'

'Thair hes bene greit abusion of justice in the north partis and west partis of the realm sic as the north Ilies and south Ilis. And therethrough, the pepill ar almaist gane wild.' – Notes from Parliament, 1504.

GRAND LARCENY: THE GREAT RAID

The Grant chieftain James of the Raids was no match for the Clan Donald force that descended on Urquhart in April or May 1545.

This was perhaps the most audacious – and certainly the best documented – of all Highland raids. The MacDonalds held the castle for several weeks, and a staggering amount was taken (see opposite). Despite earlier raids, Urquhart was clearly very wealthy at the time of the Great Raid.

The raid's leaders were eventually beheaded and the Grants sought compensation for the damage to their lands. The castle was subsequently rebuilt, but the Great Glen and Urquhart remained unstable.

As a fragile peace returned to the glen, the Grants began to repair the ravaged castle. Work continued into the following century.

Left Raiders from Clan Donald shown stripping Urquhart Castle of assets.

The raiders took an enormous haul of booty from the castle and its estates, which included:

- 3 great boats
- 3,377 sheep
- 2,355 cattle
- 2,204 goats
- 395 horses
- 122 swine
- 64 geese
- 3,206 bolls (1,700 sacks) of oats
- 1,427 bolls (750 sacks) of bere barley
- 60 ells (56m) of cloth
- 2 brewing vats
- 6 roasting spits
- 5 pots and 6 pans
- a chest containing £300
- 20 artillery pieces, with gunpowder
- stands of armour
- doors, locks and yetts (iron gates)
- 12 feather beds with bolsters, blankets and sheets, tables and other items of furniture, to a total value of £323

ENGLISH INTERFERENCE?

The raid may have been sponsored by Henry VIII of England *(above)*, who had formed an alliance with Clan Donald. Henry seems to have viewed the raid as an opportunity to distract Scottish forces while he launched a military campaign via the Clyde – although that scheme was never brought to fruition.

This was during a period known as 'the Rough Wooing', when Scotland was destabilised by ruthless English raids, designed to coerce a contract of marriage between the infant Mary Queen of Scots and Prince Edward, heir to the English throne.

At this time, the Scottish Crown had poor relationships with the Highland chiefs, allowing opportunistic English kings to foster alliances, largely through bribery.

Gaels had a distinctive way of understanding land, identity, rights and duties through the concept of Dùthchas. It is hard to translate into English, but expresses hereditary rights, familial traditions and hereditary traits.

For Gaels, rights to farm, hunt and occupy land were closely tied up with an understanding of tradition and inherited obligation. This was at odds with legalistic interpretations of land ownership introduced by the Crown from the 1500s onwards.

HIGHLAND TRADITION: DÙTHCHAS

In 1574, Duncan Grant, 4th Laird was annoyed that his tenants at Urquhart had hunted on his land. He saw this as poaching, but for local people it was an expression of commonly understood land rights.

On one occasion, the Grants were awarded land in Easter Ross after a rising of the Islesmen. They were never able to control the land, as local people did not consider them legitimate owners. They had no Dùthchas to it.

Fighting and feasting

Raiding was an important part of Gaelic culture, particularly in a period of instability when neither the Crown nor local lords could provide order and security.

It was common for a chief to employ a small band of highly trained warriors. Warfare between these elites was a way of asserting status, honour and rights to land. Its most common form was the *togail creach* – the cattle raid. New chiefs often engaged in cattle theft to prove their mettle: this was regarded as a traditional practice rather than robbery.

It was understood that goods seized in warfare should be used for extravagant feasting (*left*). The chief would play host, sharing the spoils among his followers to demonstrate his status.

Cattle were an important source of wealth in the region, and were symbolically important. Marriages were often sealed with a *tochradh* or dowry of cattle.

Between periods of raiding and warfare were diplomacy and marriage. James Grant, 'Am Bard Ruadh', married a daughter of Clan Cameron, in an unsuccessful attempt to stop feuding and bring peace. The shifting allegiances of the clans reflected wider politics in Scotland and beyond, but were understood through the norms of Gaelic society.

THE KING'S ENFORCERS

One of the roles of the Grant chiefs of Urquhart was in bringing the King's Peace to the region. This meant hunting down raiders and bandits – and occasionally an errant cousin.

There was a longstanding tradition – as far back as Alan Durward in the 1230s – that the keeper of Urquhart Castle also served as sheriff of Inverness. This is perhaps unsurprising, given the lawless nature of the vast territory of Urquhart.

The Grant family were also sheriffs of Inverness before being given the castle. This role, as 'enforcer' for the Gordon earls of Huntly, and often for the Crown, was to continue into the 1600s.

The Grants wasted no time in trying to bring order to the region. John Grant seized the bandits Alan Mór McEwan and Finlay Gibbonson in 1498–9, for which he was rewarded by the Crown.

Over the years, the Grant chiefs were involved in the pursuit and capture of several famous bandits in the area. They included Gavin Cuim – the Halket Stirk (Scots: 'Streaky Calf') – and Gille Ruaidh (another 'Red-Haired Lad') – also known as Gilderoy – whose infamy had spread as far as London.

Another notorious brigand brought in by a Grant chief was his own cousin Seaumas an Tuim ('James of the Hillock'). A rather unlikely legend says Seaumas later escaped from Edinburgh Castle using a rope hidden in a pat of butter.

Left The persistent bandit Seaumas an Tuim brought before his cousin the Grant chief at Urquhart Castle.

While the Grant chiefs were often rewarded for bringing outlaws to justice, they were sometimes blamed for failing to apprehend wrongdoers, especially when they were themselves Grants. In 1631 Sir John Grant earned a rebuke from King Charles I when word of banditry in the area became so notorious it reached the royal court.

THE RAIDER'S LAMENT

This extract is from a song attributed to Domhnall Donn, a cattle thief of the late 1600s who was apprehended by the Grant laird.

Nam biodh fios mi bhith 'n-sàs
Gun dùil ri fuasgladh gu bràth,
'S lìonmhor ghabhadh mo phàirt 's
an uair seo.

'S iomadh maighdeann glan ùr,
Chluinnteadh faram a gùin,
A chuireadh na crùin gu m' fhuasgladh.

If they would know I was captive/with no expectation of release/many would take my part at this time./Many a bright young maiden/whose gown would be heard to rustle/would give crowns to release me.

1

2

NATIONAL STRUGGLES AND LOCAL FEUDS

The Grants moved among the upper ranks of Scottish society, but their involvement in national affairs was often underpinned by local interests.

Like other clan chiefs, they were not simply local warlords; they were closely involved with politics at court and across Europe.

However, when Highland chiefs became involved in national events, they were often driven in part by clan rivalries. This helps explain the exploits of the Grant lairds.

1   The coat of arms of Mary Grant,
     landlord of Urquhart.

2   Her son James, 7th Laird, and his
     wife, Lady Mary Stewart.

John Grant, 6th Laird, died in 1637. His 21-year-old son, James Grant, became 7th Laird, but it was John's widow, Mary, who came to live at the castle. Perhaps unavoidably, Lady Grant and her son became involved both in local disputes, and in the national struggle between the Crown and the Covenanters.

In 1638, James Grant, 7th Laird, signed the National Covenant, resisting attempts by King Charles I to reform religious practice in Scotland. In the civil war that followed, Grant's loyalties proved fickle. In 1643 he refused to endorse the Solemn League and Covenant, demanding the establishment of Presbyterian worship in Scotland. Grant now joined the Royalist faction.

3

At Christmas 1644, Urquhart Castle was attacked by a band of Covenanters from Inverness, assisted by some of the Grants' tenants. According to local legend, Mary Grant was expelled from the castle, which was ransacked.

In 1647, James Grant commissioned an inventory of the furnishings remaining at his castle: a few beds, tables, benches, chairs and an old chest. Aside from that it was 'without any kynd of uther wairis, pleneishing, goodies or geir whatsumever'. The total value was £20. Undeterred, Grant spent a considerable sum on repairs.

3 A painting of the 1800s depicting the signing of the National Covenant.
4 The National Covenant itself.

A HIGHLAND GARRISON

Urquhart became a significant focus for military activity during the first Jacobite Rising of 1689 – but again, the larger conflict was indistinguishable from feuding between rival Highland clans.

1

On a national level, this upheaval arose from the 'Glorious Revolution' of 1688, which had ousted the exiled Catholic King James VII in favour of his Protestant daughter Mary and her Dutch husband, William of Orange.

In support of the new monarchs, Colonel Ludovick Grant, 8th Laird, raised an infantry regiment – mostly kinsmen from his own estate – and used this force to garrison several strongholds, including Urquhart.

In December 1689, fewer than 100 of his men repelled an attack on the castle by a much larger Jacobite force. The besiegers were led by MacDonell of Glengarry, but mostly composed of Camerons. For them, this was largely another chapter in the centuries-old feud between Grant and Cameron – only notionally related to the wider civil war.

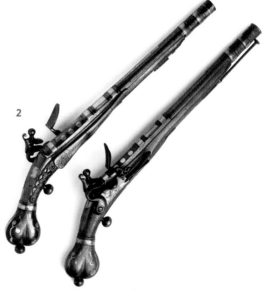

2

1 Colonel Ludovick Grant, 8th Laird of Freuchie.
2 A pair of pistols owned by Ludovick Grant.

THE 'DAMNIFICATION' OF URQUHART

As the first Jacobite Rising continued, Urquhart Castle found a new role as a base for professional soldiers. This was ultimately to prove its undoing.

In 1690, Grant's men at Urquhart were joined or replaced by regular soldiers of the Crown, who were presumably less concerned with local clan rivalries. Urquhart saw little direct action after 1689, but it had played an important role in protecting government supply lines along the Great Glen.

The story goes that when the troops departed in 1693 they blew up the gatehouse, rendering the castle impossible to defend if the Jacobites tried to occupy it. There is no hard evidence to support this account, but the south gatehouse tower certainly collapsed.

In any case, more than three years as an army barracks had left Urquhart largely uninhabitable. Grant filed a compensation claim, complaining that 'soldiers of His Majesty's regular forces' were responsible for 'damnifying' his property. The castle was never repaired.

3 The collapsed south gatehouse tower.

A NOBLE RUIN

No longer usable as a noble residence, Urquhart soon declined. But as attitudes changed, the medieval castle came to be viewed as a noble ruin in a majestic setting.

When the last garrison marched out in 1693, the castle buildings rapidly fell into decay.

People from the glen came and salvaged what they could for use elsewhere – the best of the stonework, the lead from the roofs, the timber and the ironwork.

On 19 February 1715, part of the Grant Tower came crashing to the ground during a violent storm, leaving a gaping hole in one side of the building.

A survey of the castle and grounds made about 1770 shows the ancient castle buildings roofless, but someone was living in a long, narrow building immediately beyond the castle ditch, close to where the large kiln remains today. The building lay at the corner of a large garden.

In the early 1800s, encouraged by the writings of Sir Walter Scott and others, people began to take a greater interest in ruined castles, beyond their value as salvage yards. Set against one of the most dramatic of Highland landscapes, Urquhart Castle drew an increasing number of visitors, to gaze in awe, to think on times past, to sketch and to paint.

1 A print of the castle from a book of the 1850s.
2 Samuel Taylor Coleridge.
3 Robert Burns.

BY ANY OTHER NAME

Lairds of the castle were known to their tenants as *fithich dhuba* ('black ravens') – apparently referring to their appetite for the food produced in the glen. By the 1800s, the castle was often referred to as Strome or Strone Castle. This is derived from the Gaelic, Caisteal na Sròine ('the Castle on the Headland').

They included the Scottish poet Robert Burns and the English poet Samuel Taylor Coleridge, who viewed the castle from the military road on the far side of the loch. At that time the castle was difficult to access and more often viewed from this remote location.

The English artist J.M.W. Turner made a number of pencil sketches of the castle in 1831, but does not seem to have completed a finished illustration or full-scale painting. But when John Everett Millais visited in 1878, following the death of his son, he produced a melancholic painting of the ruins (see page 70).

2

3

In 1884, Ian Charles Ogilvy-Grant, 8th Earl of Seafield died. His mother Caroline, the dowager countess, assumed control of his estates, including Urquhart and Glenmoriston. When she died, in 1911, her will instructed that Urquhart's fragile ruins be entrusted into State care.

On 6 October 1912, a guardianship agreement was signed, transferring responsibility for the castle's upkeep to the Commissioners of His Majesty's Works and Public Buildings. Historic Environment Scotland, as successor to that body, continues to maintain the ancient ruins to this day.

4 John Everett Millais.
5 Millais's Urquhart painting, 'The Tower of Strength'.

FURTHER READING

- N. Bridgland, *Urquhart Castle and the Great Glen* (2005)
- M. Brown, *The Wars of Scotland 1214–1371* (2010)
- E.J. Cowan and L. Henderson (eds), *A History of Everyday Life in Medieval Scotland 1000–1600* (2011)
- R. Dodgshon, *The Age of the Clans: The Highlands from Somerled to the Clearances* (2002)
- R. Dodgshon, *From Chiefs to Landlords: Social and Economic Change in the Western Highlands and Islands, c.1493–1820* (1998)
- Sir W. Fraser, *The Chiefs of Grant* (3 vols) (1883)
- J. Gifford, *The Buildings of Scotland: Highlands and Islands* (1992)
- W. MacKay, *Urquhart and Glenmoriston* (1914)
- M. Newton, *Warriors of the Word: The World of the Scottish Highlanders* (2009)
- R. Oram, *The Kings and Queens of Medieval Scotland* (2004)
- W.D. Simpson, 'Urquhart Castle' in *Transactions of the Gaelic Society of Inverness*, vol. 35 (1930)

Right A portrait by Richard Waitt of the Laird of Grant's piper, William Cumming.

CREDITS

This edition first published by Historic Environment Scotland 2022
Printed from sustainable materials
© Historic Environment Scotland 2022

Historic Environment Scotland
Scottish Charity No. SC045925

Principal Office
Longmore House, Salisbury Place, Edinburgh EH9 1SH

Authors Kevin Grant, Rachel Pickering and Nicki Scott
Design Stand stand.agency
Photography Historic Environment Scotland Photo Unit
Heraldic illustrations p.4, 34, 35 cr, 36, 50 and 64: Yvonne Holton
Illustrations p. 8, 10, 16, 19, 22–23, 24–25, 34 and **inside back cover:** Stephen Conlin/Pictu Ltd
Illustrations p. 30, 36 bl, 37 cl, and 58: David Simon
Illustrations p. 42, 47, 52, 60–61, 62: David Lawrence
Illustration p.46: Phil Kenning

ISBN 978-1-84917-305-6

URQUHART CASTLE AT A GLANCE

1 Summit enclosure
The main focus of the earliest stone castle until the late 1200s.
p.8

2 Upper Bailey
The site of stables and workshops from the 1300s.
p.10

3 Doocot
The remains of a beehive-shaped building where pigeons were housed.
p.12

4 Smithy?
Ruins of a building that may have been a smithy at some point in its life.
p.10

5 Water Gate
Providing access to the loch at a time when water was the most efficient route for travel.
p.12

6 Gatehouse
A well-defended entrance to the castle.
p.14

7 Ditch
Cut from solid rock to help defend the castle's vulnerable landward side.
p.18

8 Site of Drawbridge
The drawbridge allowed access to the castle but could be bolted closed in case of attack.
p.18

9 Nether Bailey
A courtyard providing access to the great hall, chapel and associated buildings.
p.21

10 Chapel?
Ruins of two small rectangular buildings, either of which may have been the castle's chapel.
p.22

11 Great Hall Cellars
The great hall was the main public room of the castle. Only the cellar level, used for storage, now survives.
p.24

12 Great Kitchens
Where food was prepared for banquets in the great hall.
p.27

13 Inner Close
A courtyard for secondary buildings associated with the Grant Tower.
p.28

14 Kitchen?
This may have been the Grant Tower's kitchen.
p.28

15 Grant Tower/Donjon
A fashionable five-storey tower house, built in the mid-1500s as the castle's main residence.
p.30

16 Site of Castletoun
Once filled with life and noise, as the craftsmen serving the castle's residents went about their business.
p.20

17 Kiln
A furnace associated with later occupation of the site.

♦♦ Toilets
⊖ Cafe
P Parking